I0748451

Published by Angelis Publications
ISBN: 978-1-912484-32-4
www.angelispublications.com

In Loving Memory of

"Life is eternal,
and love is immortal,
and death is only a horizon;
and a horizon is nothing
save the limit of our sight."

Rossiter Worthington Raymond

Name / Address

Thoughts & Memories

Name / Address

Thoughts & Memories

Name / Address

Thoughts & Memories

Name / Address

Thoughts & Memories

Name / Address

Thoughts & Memories

Name / Address

Thoughts & Memories

Name / Address

Thoughts & Memories

Name / Address

Thoughts & Memories

Name / Address

Thoughts & Memories

Name / Address

Thoughts & Memories

Name / Address

Thoughts & Memories

Name / Address

Thoughts & Memories

Name / Address

Thoughts & Memories

Name / Address

Thoughts & Memories

Name / Address

Thoughts & Memories

Name / Address

Thoughts & Memories

Name / Address

Thoughts & Memories

Name / Address

Thoughts & Memories

Name / Address

Thoughts & Memories

Name / Address

Thoughts & Memories

Name / Address

Thoughts & Memories

Name / Address

Thoughts & Memories

Name / Address

Thoughts & Memories

Name / Address

Thoughts & Memories

Name / Address

Thoughts & Memories

Name / Address

Thoughts & Memories

Name / Address

Thoughts & Memories

Name / Address

Thoughts & Memories

Name / Address

Thoughts & Memories

Name / Address

Thoughts & Memories

Name / Address

Thoughts & Memories

Name / Address

Thoughts & Memories

Name / Address

Thoughts & Memories

Name / Address

Thoughts & Memories

Name / Address

Thoughts & Memories

Name / Address

Thoughts & Memories

Name / Address

Thoughts & Memories

Name / Address

Thoughts & Memories

Name / Address

Thoughts & Memories

Name / Address

Thoughts & Memories

Name / Address

Thoughts & Memories

Name / Address

Thoughts & Memories

Name / Address

Thoughts & Memories

Name / Address

Thoughts & Memories

Name / Address

Thoughts & Memories

Name / Address

Thoughts & Memories

Name / Address

Thoughts & Memories

Name / Address

Thoughts & Memories

Name / Address

Thoughts & Memories

Name / Address

Thoughts & Memories

Name / Address

Thoughts & Memories

Name / Address

Thoughts & Memories

Name / Address

Thoughts & Memories

Name / Address

Thoughts & Memories

Name / Address

Thoughts & Memories

Name / Address

Thoughts & Memories

Name / Address

Thoughts & Memories

Name / Address

Thoughts & Memories

Name / Address

Thoughts & Memories

Name / Address

Thoughts & Memories

Name / Address

Thoughts & Memories

Name / Address

Thoughts & Memories

Name / Address

Thoughts & Memories

Name / Address

Thoughts & Memories

Name / Address

Thoughts & Memories

Name / Address

Thoughts & Memories

Name / Address

Thoughts & Memories

Name / Address

Thoughts & Memories

Name / Address

Thoughts & Memories

Name / Address

Thoughts & Memories

Name / Address

Thoughts & Memories

Name / Address

Thoughts & Memories

Name / Address

Thoughts & Memories

Name / Address

Thoughts & Memories

Name / Address

Thoughts & Memories

Name / Address

Thoughts & Memories

Name / Address

Thoughts & Memories

Name / Address

Thoughts & Memories

Name / Address

Thoughts & Memories

Name / Address

Thoughts & Memories

Name / Address

Thoughts & Memories

Name / Address

Thoughts & Memories

Name / Address

Thoughts & Memories

Name / Address

Thoughts & Memories

Name / Address

Thoughts & Memories

Name / Address

Thoughts & Memories

Name / Address

Thoughts & Memories

Name / Address

Thoughts & Memories

Name / Address

Thoughts & Memories

Name / Address

Thoughts & Memories

Name / Address

Thoughts & Memories

Name / Address

Thoughts & Memories

Name / Address

Thoughts & Memories

Name / Address

Thoughts & Memories

www.ingramcontent.com/pod-product-compliance
Lightning Source LLC
Chambersburg PA
CBHW081126300726
48982CB00005B/862

* 9 7 8 1 9 1 2 4 8 4 3 2 4 *